1/11

THE GREAT ARTISTS
& THEIR WORLD
MANET

New
Forest
Press

Publisher: Melissa Fairley
Editor: Guy Croton
Designer: Carol Davis
Production Controller: Ed Green
Production Manager: Suzy Kelly

ISBN: 978-1-84898-313-7
Library of Congress Control Number: 2010925213
Tracking number: nfp0004

North American edition copyright © TickTock Entertainment Ltd. 2010
First published in North America in 2010 by New Forest Press,
PO Box 784, Mankato, MN 56002
www.newforestpress.com

Printed in the USA
9 8 7 6 5 4 3 2 1

CONTENTS

INTRODUCTION

In many ways, modern art started with Édouard Manet. Before he began exhibiting, most artists knew that to become well-known and successful, they had to paint in a certain way—this included portraying conventional subjects, using smooth brush marks, and making their paintings look as realistic as possible. Manet's work broke those rules. His paintings of contemporary events and people were considered vulgar and his emphasis on sketchy paint application using bold colors and brushwork shocked the art establishment. What audacity! What disrespect! What was he thinking?

REJECTION

He was thinking, actually, that art needed to change. For too long, he considered, it had been stuck in a rut, with art officials deciding what was suitable and what was not and artists themselves not having a say in what they should do. Manet felt that art had become dull and unrelated to modern life and although his unconventional paintings horrified the art establishment, they gave confidence to other modern-thinking artists such as the future Impressionists. Once he had led the way, these artists felt it was acceptable to portray subjects of their own choice expressively and individually, instead of always depicting long-established themes and trying to make their paintings look as highly finished as possible.

The first of Manet's pictures that caused uproar was *Le Déjeuner sur l'Herbe* ("Luncheon on the Grass") of 1863. It was rejected by the official annual art exhibition in Paris and exhibited instead at the Salon des Refusés (the exhibition of rejected art). Portraying a naked woman sitting between two fully clothed men was shocking enough, but in addition, the paint was sketchy and the work did not look realistic, as Manet had deliberately flattened the forms. But Manet did not see himself as a revolutionary—he believed he was continuing traditions of the Old Masters. When critics described his work as unskilled and offensive, he was hurt, but instead of trying to please them by painting time-honored historical or mythological subjects, he continued depicting the world around him using his avant-garde technique, featuring bright colors, lack of detail, and changing scales and proportions.

PERCEPTIVE OBSERVATIONS

Throughout his career, with his style and methods, Manet could not be categorized. He was always too full of contradictions. For instance, he admired the methods and subjects of Old Masters, yet he painted modern life, he socialized with the Impressionists but never exhibited with them, he painted a range of subjects, including

landscapes, portraits, everyday scenes, and still lifes but also scenes of history that conventional artists painted (although he did this in his unconventional style). He was an accomplished draughtsman, a skilled printmaker, and he could use pastels as proficiently as he painted. His astute observations of the people, places, and events he saw around him were his main inspirations and this was considered one of his greatest mistakes by the French art academy—modern life was deemed too unsightly for art. Traditional artists tried to convey permanence and solidity but Manet created a sense of spontaneity. The new ideas he introduced and the prejudices he overcame helped to make him recognized as one of the most original and influential painters of the nineteenth century and a key figure in the development of modern art.

SPANISH INFLUENCE

Coming from a wealthy family, Manet did not need to
earn his living from painting, but throughout his life he
longed for recognition by the French art authorities and
was always shocked by the scandal his paintings provoked
and his lack of success. He aimed to learn as much as he
could from the great masters before him and in the 1850s,
he traveled to study art in Holland, Germany, Prague,
Italy, and Austria. Ten years later, he visited Spain where
the work of Velázquez (1599–1660) in particular had a
powerful effect on him. From then on, he began to
incorporate some of the Spanish master's ideas in
his work, including featuring dramatic viewpoints
and Spanish subjects and using black to enhance the
contrasts of light. He spent many hours in the Louvre in Paris,
studying the work of Spanish artists above all and at one
point, he was nicknamed "the Spanish Parisian."

THE WORLD OF THE 1860s

We have all of us got the republican spirit in our veins, as we have the pox in our bones"—Charles Baudelaire. Baudelaire, the French poet, critic, and friend of Édouard Manet, was convinced that art should be about *la vie moderne* (modern life), not mythology, or history. Art should be rooted in reality, the reality of modern man who fought in the Paris revolution in 1848; who worked in the factories of the great industrial nations such as England, France, and Germany; who built the railways and ships that were expanding the wealth of trading nations around the world; who fought in America for the right to be free from slavery. He believed that art, like science, should reveal the truth. Art should be a mirror held up to the world, showing men and women as they really were—the beggar, the alcoholic, the shop girl, the prostitute. Artists such as Courbet and Manet were searching for a new realism, seeking to represent the "heroism of modern life."

EVOLUTION

Charles Darwin wrote a book that shocked the world when it was published in 1859. The book was called *On the Origin of Species.* It explained that humans and animals had gradually evolved over millions of years as a result of a process of natural selection, which favored those creatures best adapted to suit the conditions in which they lived.

President Lincoln's Union army fought for the abolition of slavery, which still kept millions of African-Americans in forced labor. The North was victorious and the war was over by April 1865. Despite the abolition of slavery, most slaves could not integrate into a society which still did not tolerate them.

THE REVOLUTIONARY THINKER

Exiled from his home country of Germany, Karl Marx moved to England in 1849, where he developed his ideas about the economics of capitalism and class struggle. In 1867, his theories were published in a book entitled *Das Kapital* which was to become the communist "bible." Marx believed that the struggle between the rich rulers and the poor workers would result in revolution, and that the workers would overthrow their masters: *"the workers have nothing to lose but their chains."* Marx died in London in 1883. In 1917, the Russian revolution established the first communist state based on his ideas.

THE TRADE CANAL

The Suez Canal cuts through 100 miles of Egyptian mainland linking the Mediterranean Sea and the Red Sea. It took ten years to build with French help and opened in 1869. The canal enabled shipping to avoid the long journey south around the African continent, cutting over 7,000 miles from the distance that ships needed to sail to reach the Far East.

FREE TRADE?

Western European powers had forced the unwilling Chinese to open their frontiers to trade in the 1840s. After the seizure of a British ship and the murder of a missionary, an armed Anglo-French expedition was sent to bombard Canton in retaliation. Armed skirmishes continued as the Chinese continued to resist the European imperial presence and in 1859, the British burned the Chinese Imperial Summer Palace. This pressure eventually forced China to sign a treaty opening up eleven Chinese ports to foreign trade.

FIGHTING FOR FREEDOM

The United States of America was rapidly expanding throughout the 19th century. In 1845, Texas joined the Union; in 1848 California was added and European immigrants swelled the population to ever higher numbers. In 1860, Abraham Lincoln was elected president, prompting the state of South Carolina to declare independence. The following year more Southern states left the Union and civil war erupted between the Northern Union and the Confederacy of the Southern states.

THE WORLD OF MANET

ÉDOUARD MANET

Édouard Manet was born in Paris on January 23, 1832, the eldest of three sons born to Auguste Manet and Eugénie Désirée Fournier. Édouard was urged by his father to take up a career in the legal profession but his interests were in art, not law. Art was not an acceptable career as far as Auguste Manet was concerned; instead Édouard applied to join the naval college, but failed the entrance examination. He then joined the Merchant Marine, and in 1848 set sail on the training ship *Le Havre et Guadeloupe*, bound for Brazil. Manet describes the journey in detail in his letters home. He was shocked at what he saw in Rio de Janeiro. *"In this country all the negroes are slaves; they all look downtrodden; it's extraordinary what power the whites have over them; I saw a slave market, a rather revolting spectacle for people like us."* France had abolished slavery in its Caribbean colonies in March of the previous year.

When the young Manet arrived back in France in 1849, he was determined to become an artist and his father relented, allowing him to enroll at the studio of the artist Thomas Couture in Paris. Manet was to enjoy the life of the Parisian *flâneur* (stroller). This meant a person of sophistication and elegance, a dandy with white gloves, top hat, and cane, who strolled the boulevards and mixed with the bohemian painters, writers, and composers in the many fashionable cafés. The word *rentier* also applied to Manet. This meant a person of private financial means who was free, as Manet was, to indulge in his desires rather than needing to work for his living.

BRAZILIAN SCENES

Manet felt no embarrassment in communicating his feelings about the Brazilian peoples and their habits. In a letter to his mother Manet writes: *"most Brazilian women are very pretty: they have superb dark eyes and hair to match... they never go out alone but are always followed by their black maid or accompanied by their children... The Carnival of Rio is something quite special... At 3 o'clock all the Brazilian ladies are at their front doors or on their balconies, bombarding every gentleman who passes by with multicolored wax balls filled with water; these are called limons. My pockets were filled with limons and I gave as good as I got, which is the proper thing to do."*

THE BARRICADE, 1871

*Manet's Observation of
the Streets of Paris*

It was clear from letters home from Brazil in 1848 that Manet was a republican. On that occasion he wrote to his father *"Try to keep for our return a healthy Republic."* When France made the disastrous move of declaring war on Prussia in 1870, the French army was quickly over-run and Paris was under siege. Manet joined the National Guard. He recorded: *"We're beginning to feel the pinch here, horsemeat is a delicacy, donkey is exorbitantly expensive, there are butcher's shops for dogs, cats, and rats..."* But worse was to follow. The defeat led to conflict between the Parisian National Guard and the army resulting in civil war. The suppression of the Paris Commune in 1871 led to the death of over 20,000 Communards. The English journalist Archibald Forbes wrote: *"Europe professes civilization and France boasts of culture and Frenchmen are braining one another with the butt end of muskets, and Paris is burning."*

BULLFIGHT, 1865/66

Manet visited Madrid in 1865, and fell under the spell of Spanish painting. The work of Spanish artists such as Velázquez and Goya had a profound influence on Manet's own style of painting and choice of subject matter. Spanish fashion was very popular in Paris at this time with the Louvre art gallery acquiring works by Spanish artists, and popular entertainment such as the Ambassadeurs Theater playing Spanish dance troupes nightly. Manet developed this picture from the sketches he made while attending bullfights in Spain.

9

ROMANS OF THE DECADENCE

Thomas Couture

The teaching of art in France was the responsibility of the Écoles des Beaux-Arts. The Écoles (schools) taught according to principles set by the Academies almost 200 years earlier: Academies existed to preserve traditions, not to create new ones. The Romanticism of Delacroix had begun to shake the foundations of the establishment of the Academies; their view of classical art as representing the image of moral beauty in physical perfection, and as a means of redirecting the mind to purer things was becoming outdated. Manet did not want to study at the Écoles. Instead he paid 120 francs a year for tuition from Thomas Couture, who was an artist with an excellent reputation whose classical subjects were painted with a modern touch.

Fantin-Latour, Champfleury, Manet, Baudelaire. Alphonse Legros, Felix Bracquemond, and Edmond Duranty are also shown but not identified.

HOMAGE TO DELACROIX

Henri Fantin-Latour

The artistic and literary set that Manet mixed with in Paris are represented in this painting by Henri Fantin-Latour. It is called *Homage to Delacroix*, because Delacroix's portrait is shown in the center of the painting. Delacroix had said that if an artist lacked the skill to draw a man falling out of a fifth floor window in the time it takes for him to hit the ground he would never produce a "monumental" work. Critics have pointed out, however, that none of those depicted is actually looking at the portrait of Delacroix. The critic Jean Rousseau expressed the view that the painting was devoted to the *glory of realism*.

THE BIRTH OF VENUS

Alexandre Cabanel

It was every artist's ambition to have his work exhibited in the Salon in Paris. The female nude was a popular subject, particularly when it was represented in an acceptable way such as Cabanel's painting of the Venus creation myth, despite its overt eroticism. The Salon was crucial to an artist because there was no real alternative place of exhibition for an artist's work.

THE ART OF HIS DAY

French art in the first half of the 19th century had been dominated by the Romantic painter Eugène Delacroix, who had turned to contemporary and exotic literary references, such as Byron, for subject matter instead of the classical approach favored by French academicians. The artist Gustave Courbet rejected any notion of idealization in art, rejecting both classicism and romanticism in favor of a natural representation of everyday life. Courbet stated that only realism was really democratic and that the noblest subject for the artist to paint was the peasant and worker. Manet's own particular style took on board the influence of Spanish art and Impressionist technique but owed much to Courbet's dedication to realism.

THE BARGE (MONET PAINTING ON HIS STUDIO BOAT), 1874 *(detail)*

Monet was influenced and encouraged by Manet who introduced him to the artistic circles in Paris. Monet recalled that in 1869, Manet invited him to a café in the Batignolles area where he and his friends met every evening after leaving their studios. Some years later Monet was to persuade Manet to work *en plein air* painting out of doors in the "fresh air" instead of in his studio.

THE PAINTER'S STUDIO

Gustave Courbet

This monumental picture has a title to match, *The Painter's Studio: A Real Allegory Summing up Seven Years of My Artistic Life*. It was painted by Courbet in 1855, at the height of his fame. The figures in the painting are about life size, so big is the canvas, and represent specific people and types. Courbet's friends such as Baudelaire and the Realist writer Champfleury are included along with allegorical figures, such as truth (the naked woman is the naked truth, meaning art should be true to life), and the untutored, innocent eyes of youth examining Courbet's landscape.

PORTRAIT OF MONSIEUR
AND MADAME MANET, 1860

A few days after the birth of his first son, Auguste Manet was named a Chevalier of the Légion of Honor. This honor, along with the birth of a son, must have brought happiness to the Manet household. The following year a second son was born and named Eugene. Two years later a third son, Gustave, was born to the Manets. Eugénie was 20 years old when she married Auguste, 14 years younger than her husband. In 1857, three years before this portrait was painted, Auguste was stricken with paralysis. He was unable to use his legs for over a year and he lost the power of speech, causing him to resign from his post of judge at the Court of the First Instance. Auguste died in 1862, but Eugénie was to outlive her eldest son by two years.

FAMILY, FRIENDS, & OTHERS

Édouard Manet was born on January 23, 1832 into a prosperous middle-class family who were university-educated landowners. His father, Auguste Manet, followed his own father's footsteps into a career as a magistrate and judge, and expected his first born son Édouard to do the same. The Manets were the very picture of respectability, a model Parisian family. Manet's mother, Eugénie Désirée, was the goddaughter of the Crown Prince of Sweden. She brought with her a considerable dowry as well as perhaps even greater social standing. The family lived in an imposing four story apartment house at 5, Rue Bonaparte near the Seine. Manet attended Canon Poiloup's school when he was six years old, moving on to the College Rollin, a boarding school, at 12.

FRIENDS IN HIGH PLACES

Manet and Antonin Proust became friends when they met at school. Proust studied painting with Manet at Couture's studio before he decided to become a journalist. They remained lifelong friends. Manet painted this portrait in 1880, when Proust had been appointed Minister of Fine Arts.

Portrait of Antonin Proust, 1877 (detail).

LEON THE UNRECOGNIZED SON

Was Leon the illegitimate son of Édouard Manet? All the evidence suggests that this is the case, although some think that he might have been Auguste Manet's son rather than Édouard's. It is difficult to believe, however, that Manet would have lived with and later married the mother of his father's son. Manet rented an apartment for Suzanne and Leon until their marriage, after which they lived together. For the sake of appearances and fear of becoming social outcasts, Suzanne never outwardly recognized Leon as her son, and it seems that he was unaware that his own name and parentage were false until he was 20 years old. When Manet died he specified in his will that his estate should pass to his wife Suzanne, and then to Leon. In 1900, a year before her death, Suzanne finally recognized Leon as her son so that he might benefit from her inheritance. Even then she never made public the name of Leon's father.

THE LIFE OF MANET

~1832~
Édouard Manet born on January 23

~1848~
Manet joined the Merchant Marine and went to Brazil

~1849~
Returned to Paris and enrolled at the studio of Thomas Couture. Met Suzanne Leenhoff

~1852~
Leon born on January 29

~1862~
Manet's father died. Met Victorine Meurent

SUZANNE

Suzanne Leenhoff had moved from her native town of Zaltbommel in Holland to Paris at the early age of 19, making her living as a piano teacher. In 1849, the 17 year-old Manet met Suzanne when she was hired by Manet's mother to teach her sons to play the piano. At some point they became lovers, after which Suzanne hurriedly disappeared to Holland. She later returned, having given birth to a son named Leon, who was born on January 29, 1852, almost 20 years to the day after Manet's birth. An illegitimate child was unacceptable to a family of Manet's standing so Leon was passed off as Manet's godson and younger brother of Suzanne. When Suzanne returned she lived with her grandmother, son Leon, and two younger brothers, almost certainly with the financial support of the Manet family. Suzanne and Manet were not married until 1863, the year after the death of Manet's father. This portrait was begun in 1865, when she was 35 years old. It is painted in cool grays and whites but is nevertheless a tender and affectionate portrayal. Standing behind Suzanne is her son, Leon. He was added to the painting several years later, which explains why he looks older than he should have been at the time the painting was made.

THE LIFE OF MANET

~1863~
Manet and Suzanne Leenhoff are married.
Le Déjeuner sur l'Herbe exhibited

~1865~
Visited Madrid and saw paintings by Velázquez and Goya.
Olympia exhibited

~1867~
Execution of Maximilian, Emperor of Mexico. Manet holds his own exhibition on Avenue Montaigne

~1868~
Met Berthe Morisot

~1869~
Manet invited Claude Monet to a café to meet fellow artists

~1870~
France declared war on Prussia

~1871~
The Paris Commune defeated

~1873~
Met Stephané Mallarmé

~1881~
A Bar at the Folies-Bergère exhibited

~1883~
Death of Manet on April 30

~1901~
Death of Suzanne Leenhoff

PORTRAIT OF STÉPHANE MALLARMÉ, 1876

Manet met Mallarmé, an English teacher, in October 1873. Mallarmé taught at a school near the Gare Saint Lazare and lived on the rue de Moscou, not far from Manet's studio on the rue de Saint Petersbourg. Mallarmé was already having some success as a poet when Manet first knew him, and the two became close friends. Manet illustrated some of Mallarmé's publications, including his translation of Edgar Allan Poe's *The Raven*. In 1881, Manet wrote to Mallarmé: *"I feel very guilty and am afraid you may be a bit cross with me, because I've been thinking, after all, it's selfish of me not to have accepted the work you proposed—but it's also true that some of the things you suggested seem impossible, such as the woman lying in bed, seen through a window. You are a terrible lot, you poets, and it's often impossible to visualize the things you imagine."*

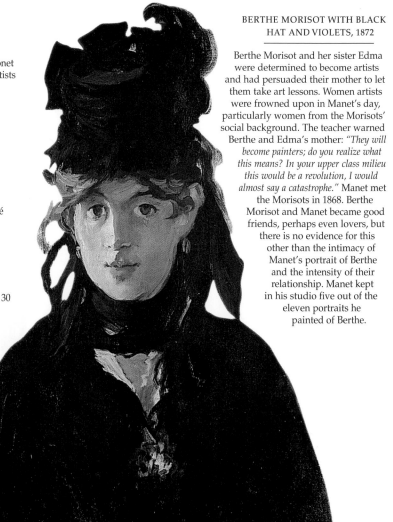

BERTHE MORISOT WITH BLACK HAT AND VIOLETS, 1872

Berthe Morisot and her sister Edma were determined to become artists and had persuaded their mother to let them take art lessons. Women artists were frowned upon in Manet's day, particularly women from the Morisots' social background. The teacher warned Berthe and Edma's mother: *"They will become painters; do you realize what this means? In your upper class milieu this would be a revolution, I would almost say a catastrophe."* Manet met the Morisots in 1868. Berthe Morisot and Manet became good friends, perhaps even lovers, but there is no evidence for this other than the intimacy of Manet's portrait of Berthe and the intensity of their relationship. Manet kept in his studio five out of the eleven portraits he painted of Berthe.

A SPECIAL FRIEND

Manet's friends, many of whom are now familiar names, mixed in the artistic and literary circles which inhabited the sophisticated café life of Paris. Manet would sit long into the evening, discussing art with the younger painters who looked up to him as leader of the revolt against the old values of the French art world. Artists such as Claude Monet, Alfred Sisley, and Auguste Renoir who were to lead the Impressionist revolution, received Manet's support although he was careful not to include himself in their Impressionist group. Though he was happy to play the part of modern master, Manet did in fact care for and sought approval from the traditional art establishment. He desperately wanted his paintings to be accepted by the *Salon* and be met with critical acclaim.

THE BALCONY, 1868/69

During 1868 Manet started work on a group portrait entitled *The Balcony*. It was exhibited at the Salon in 1869, receiving the usual critical response, one caricature was accompanied by the words: *"Do close that window, M. Manet, what I am telling you is for your own good."* The painting concentrates very much on the seated figure of Berthe Morisot whose intense black eyes stare out of the picture. Manet had only recently met Berthe and her sister Edma, but this picture shows his fascination for her. In comparison the figure of Fanny Claus who stands next to her is hardly finished. In the background stands Manet's friend Antoine Guillemet, and intriguingly, just visible in the shadows is the face of Manet's son, Leon. Berthe went to the Salon to view the painting and found Manet: *"with his hat over his eyes, looking bewildered, he begged me to look at the painting since he did not dare to himself... He laughed uneasily, declaring at one and the same time that his painting was very bad and that it would be very successful."*

BERTHE MORISOT

Berthe Morisot broke the conventions and became a successful female artist. She was invited to join the Impressionist group by Degas in recognition of her work. This may have been a difficult decision because Manet had already turned down a similar invitation, but in 1874, she did join the group and exhibited at the independent Impressionist exhibition. This may have been a deliberate act to distance herself from the overpowering influence of Manet, and assert herself as an independent artist. In December 1874, Berthe married Manet's brother, Eugene, who resembled Manet in many ways. Manet and Berthe continued to be close friends, sharing their passion for painting.

A Young Woman by Berthe Morisot (*detail*).

THE MODEL ARTIST

Manet's favorite model was Victorine Meurent. Victorine was a native Parisian from a poor family who would have had little opportunity to mix with the likes of Manet, other than as an artist's model or perhaps as a prostitute. It was a fact of life in the 1860s, that men such as Manet did not encounter women such as Victorine in any social sense. We know that she had worked as an artist's model for Manet's art teacher, Thomas Couture (after Manet had left the studio), as well as for other artists, and that Manet met her in 1862 when she was 18 years old—*"by chance in a crowd... and had been struck by her original and distinctive appearance"* —according to Manet's friend, Théodore Duret. Victorine was an artist in her own right, exhibiting a self-portrait at the Salon in 1876. Ironically, Manet's work was refused by the Salon that year.

PORTRAIT OF VICTORINE MEURENT

Victorine was 18 when Manet painted this portrait in 1862. She was to model for Manet on and off for the next 13 years, appearing in different guises in many of his best known paintings. It is likely that they were lovers; certainly Manet's marriage would have been no obstacle for a man of his social position, provided it was a private rather than a public affair. Victorine had striking red hair and a fair complexion. From examination of the preparatory studies of both *Le Déjeuner sur l'Herbe* (page 14/15) and *Olympia* (page 18) it is obvious that Victorine was the model, even though Manet darkened the hair coloring in the final version of both paintings. What is important about Manet's relationship with Victorine, however, is that in her face he found "truth." Manet said many times that his mission was to paint "the real truth." The portrait of Victorine shows an attractive redhead with creamy skin and light eyelashes, but she is not made to look pretty, nor is she idealized. It was Victorine's face that was so "real," literally the kind of woman you saw on the streets of Paris, that made it so shocking when Manet depicted it in paintings such as *Olympia*.

The Street Singer, 1862 (detail).

CHERRIES

In this picture Victorine is portrayed as a street singer, holding some fresh looking cherries wrapped in brown paper.

THE FACE FROM
LE DÉJEUNER SUR L'HERBE

As far as the art-going public were concerned, a painting of a naked goddess was acceptable, even if the model was the artist's mistress (so long as she was not recognizable), but a real woman painted without clothes was not a "decent" woman because what decent woman would let herself be seen without clothes? Manet broke the rules in the name of truth and modernity. Victorine had to suffer the scorn of the public and accusations of the press, which she did with fortitude.

THE FACE FROM
GARE SAINT-LAZARE

Victorine had traveled to America but in 1873 she returned, and Manet took the opportunity once more to include her in a painting. This is very different from the earlier pictures for which Victorine posed; she now wears a distant look, the book and dog sleeping on her lap tell of a more settled life, probably reflecting the cooling effect of time and separation on their relationship.

VICTORINE AS OLYMPIA

After Manet's death Victorine wrote to his widow, Suzanne, asking for money: *"You doubtless know that I posed for a large portion of his paintings, notably Olympia, his masterpiece. M. Manet was concerned about me and often said that if he sold his pictures he would set aside a gratuity for me, I was young then, and carefree. I left for America. When I returned, M. Manet, who had sold a large number of pictures... told me that a share of that was mine. I refused... and added that when I could no longer pose I would remind him of that promise. That time has come sooner than I expected."* Victorine is reported to have taken to drink, and disappeared from the scene.

WHAT DO THE PAINTINGS SAY?

Manet's good friend and fellow student, Antonin Proust, has described the moment when Manet decided to make the painting which was to become *Le Déjeuner sur l'Herbe*. According to Proust, while sitting on the banks of the Seine at the Paris suburb of Argenteuil, Manet's attention was caught by some bathers. Manet then said to Proust: *"I'm told that I must do a nude. All right, I will. I'll do them a nude. Back in our student days, I copied Giorgione's women, the women with the musicians. That's a dark picture. The background has retreated. I'm going to do it over, and do it in the transparency of the atmosphere, with figures like you see over there."* Manet's picture does refer back to earlier work by great Italian masters such as Titian (Manet referred to a painting which has since been attributed to Titian rather than Giorgione). He wanted to incorporate references to art of an earlier period to demonstrate not just his learning but that tradition can extend into modern "realist" painting.

MANET'S FAVORITE

The model for the naked woman who looks at the viewer so directly and without a trace of shame was Victorine Meurent, a professional model who Manet first met in 1862, the year before the picture was made. Victorine would have been 19 years old at the time, and had already been the subject of many of Manet's paintings. A preparatory study for the painting shows the female figure with red hair, the color of Victorine's own hair, but Manet has changed it to brown for the final version.

THE FROG

Manet added a humorous touch to this painting by including a frog in the bottom left-hand corner.

HIDDEN SIGNS

Manet clearly made art historical references to more than just the Raphael picture. The overturned basket was a symbol of the loss of innocence, fruits such as peaches, cherries, and figs were also recognized symbols and the empty oyster shells signal that the oysters, always regarded as an aphrodisiac, have already been consumed.

IN THE FAMILY

The male figure at the center of the picture was based on Ferdinand Leenhoff, brother of Suzanne Leenhoff, who became Manet's wife. The figure on the right was that of Manet's brother Eugene, who posed for the painting.

SCANDAL
AT THE SALON

Le Déjeuner sur l'Herbe was exhibited in 1863 at the Salon des Refusés, the alternative exhibition to the official Salon, and caused an immediate outcry. Manet's picture quickly became a success due to controversy; why was the woman naked but the men clothed? This was apparently a modern painting depicting a real event with men in Parisian dress having luncheon on the grass *(Déjeuner sur l'Herbe)*. Such a scene would have been acceptable if it were cloaked in the respectability of the classical tradition (not in modern dress!), but Manet had flouted tradition by painting real people in a modern world. The critic Ernest Chesneau attacked the painting, accusing Manet of trying to attain celebrity by shocking the bourgeois. Manet replied by saying that he obviously should have painted the men in the nude as well as the woman, as they would be in an old master painting. Nevertheless Manet did become a celebrity as a result of the picture.

JUDGEMENT OF PARIS

Marcantonio Raimondi

This engraving by Raimondi, after the painting by Raphael dating from around 1520, clearly shows the inspiration for the three seated figures in Manet's painting. The nakedness of the River Gods in this classical image did not offend, but Manet's version angered the critics and public alike. The critics were quick to pick up the "art historical" reference which Manet enjoyed making.

19

WHAT DO THE PAINTINGS SAY?

VIVA MEXICO

The shirt worn by Maximilian at his execution was removed and photographed. It shows the bullet holes which dealt him the final blow as he shouted *"Viva Mexico!"*

The French were the greatest foreign influence on Mexico in the 1860s. In 1863, French troops installed the Austrian Archduke Maximilian as Emperor of Mexico, following a suppression of the revolutionary republican government of Benito Juárez, which refused to recognize Mexico's debts to France, Britain, and Spain. The French thought Mexico held great mineral wealth and grimly hung on to power, fearful of American expansion. Emperor Napoleon III of France hoped to forge an alliance with Austria and to retain control over Mexico by promising the young Archduke Ferdinand 33,000 French troops to support him. At the end of the American civil war in 1865, American aid supported the ousted Juárez; at the same time Napoleon thought twice about Austria's value as an ally after it had been defeated by the Prussian army. Napoleon decided to cut his losses and withdrew his troops from Mexico, leaving the hapless Archduke Maximilian at the mercy of Juárez's army.

After the execution Maximilian's body was displayed in his coffin with black marbles replacing his eyes.

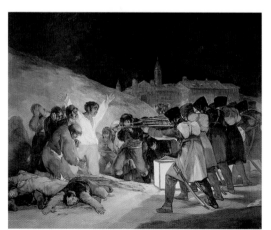

THE THIRD OF MAY

Francisco Goya

This painting which illustrates the atrocities committed by the French against the Spanish, was made by Goya in 1808. Manet would certainly have seen it when he visited Madrid in 1865, just two years before he painted the Execution of Maximilian. The similarities are striking, especially the proximity of the soldiers leveling their rifles at the victim who is at the point of death. Both Goya and Manet position the victims with arms outstretched in a Christ-like pose.

THE EXECUTION OF MAXIMILIAN

Maximilian refused to bow to Juárez's demands that he abdicate power and return home. He mistakenly believed that Europe would come to his aid and sent his wife to Paris to summon help. However, Juárez had passed a law which stated that anyone who helped foreign intervention in Mexico should face the death penalty. Maximilian was duly executed by firing squad alongside his two generals, Miramón and Mejía. In July 1867, the first news of the execution was reported in France in *Le Figaro*. Manet fell upon the subject with enthusiasm, and made several paintings on the execution theme. As more news reports of the event came back to France so Manet made changes to his pictures to suit.

FOUR PAINTINGS

Manet painted four versions of the event. The first shows the firing squad dressed in Mexican uniform, while in the last version (shown here), the uniforms resemble those of the French Imperial Guard Light Infantry, serving to illustrate how the public perception of blame had shifted from Juárez to Napoleon. The sheer brutality of the scene is conveyed in an almost journalistic way by Manet. Photographs of the incident were suppressed but verbal accounts circulated widely in the press and it is almost as if Manet illustrates the verbal accounts as a photograph might have done. The second version was cut up by Leon, Manet's son, after the artist's death. Leon considered only a part of the picture good enough to sell (the sergeant examining his rifle), which he sold to Degas. Although interest from buyers persuaded Leon to recover other portions of the picture for sale, some had already been destroyed.

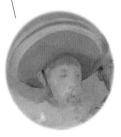

Maximilian stands in the center, wearing a sombrero, as the soldiers fire at point blank range at his general.

The soldier at the rear who appears to be casually examining his rifle is preparing to perform the final blow.

ENTRY OF NAPOLEON III INTO PARIS ON DECEMBER 2, 1852

Theodore Jung

Louis Napoleon Bonaparte became president of the Second Republic of France. His actions over the Maximilian affair brought disgrace, followed in 1870 by the collapse of the Empire.

What made matters worse as far as the critics were concerned was the fact that the real identity of *Olympia* was well known: it was Manet's favorite model, Victorine Meurent. As with *Le Déjeuner sur l'Herbe* the earlier studies for *Olympia* show quite clearly the features and red hair of Victorine. In the final painting the courtesan's hair has been toned down to dark brown.

OLYMPIA, 1863

So why were people so shocked by Manet's painting? The naked female had been painted time and again throughout the history of art and certainly was not unusual. What made Manet's *Olympia* different? She did not conform to the stereotype of the nude in art which cast women as anonymous mythical figures, handmaidens, and nymphs. Manet's woman is recognizably modern and real, and looks out at the spectator in a matter-of-fact way, directly and intimately involving the spectator in the scene. The critics and public reacted violently because they felt intimidated by *Olympia*.

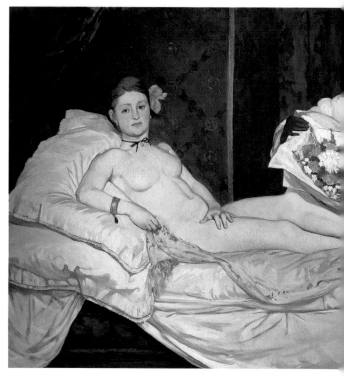

A SELF POSSESSED LADY

We are not invited to stare at *Olympia's* nakedness as part of some remote scene from a made-up history, there is no excuse or pretence for her nakedness, instead we are confronted with a modern day courtesan who is unashamed and self-possessed, aware of the power of her body. The critics could not mask their recognition of *Olympia* from their own experiences, and were angry that the real world had invaded the safe world of art.

VENUS OF URBINO *Titian*

It cannot escape notice that Manet based the composition of his painting on Titian's *Venus of Urbino*, 1538. It is known that Manet had seen and made a copy of Titian's painting on an earlier trip to Italy. Titian's *Venus* shows a seductive female who looks enticingly at the spectator, but is quite passive compared to *Olympia*.

VENUS'S DOG

At the feet of Titian's Venus lies a dog curled up and fast asleep. The dog is a well known symbol which artists use to represent faithfulness and adds a powerful message to this painting about the behavior of Venus.

WHAT DO THE PAINTINGS SAY?

Manet painted *Olympia* in 1863, the same year as *Le Déjeuner sur l'Herbe*, but did not submit it for exhibition at the *Salon* until 1865. He was undoubtedly worried about the reaction of the critics but it seemed that his friend Charles Baudelaire persuaded him to put the painting forward. Manet's fears were confirmed. The critics and public alike were baffled and outraged by Olympia. One critic said: *"I do not know whether the dictionary of French aesthetics holds expressions to characterize her... her face is stupid, her skin cadaverous."* He referred to Manet as *"a brute who paints green women with dish brushes,"* and furthermore advised young girls and pregnant women to flee *"this spectacle."* A review of the painting in *L'Artiste* continues: *"What is this Odalisque with a yellow stomach? A base model picked up I know not where, who represents Olympia? Olympia? What Olympia? A courtesan no doubt."* Manet was shattered by the criticism. He later recalled that: *"The attacks directed against me broke me in the mainspring of life. No one knows what it is to be constantly insulted. It disheartens you and undoes you."*

OLYMPIA'S CAT

In contrast to the faithful dog, Manet includes a black cat at Olympia's feet. The cat is the opposite of Venus's dog. The cat represents promiscuous behavior. The black cat became associated with Manet's name for many years after the painting was exhibited.

NANA, 1877 *(detail)*

Views did not change over time. In 1877, Manet submitted this painting to the *Salon* which rejected it as: "immoral." The subject is clearly a courtesan, and was based on the actress Henrietta Hauser, an acquaintance of Manet.

HOW WERE THEY MADE?

Manet started out working in the traditional manner of the studio based artist, making sketches and notes for paintings which were worked on in carefully controlled circumstances in his studio on the rue de Douai. The influences of the great French masters such as Delacroix and Ingres, as well as his favorite Spanish artists, contributed to his unique style which appeared more and more to highlight his subjects against a flat background, as if picked out by a spotlight against a theater backdrop. Manet never became part of the Impressionist set, even though many called him the King of Impressionism and art historians refer to Manet as the "father" of Impressionism. Manet's obsession, which was taken even further by the Impressionists, was to paint only what he saw, what appeared in front of his eyes.

LINSEED

The seeds of the flax plant yield a yellow oil, which has been used as a medium for oil painting for centuries because of its good drying properties.

OPEN AIR

In 1866, the Impressionist painter Claude Monet painted a picture entitled *Women in the Garden* entirely in the open rather than in his studio. Manet laughed at this *plein air* (open air) method of painting. Although he insisted on realism, this was going too far. After some years however, Monet's influence on Manet was apparent and Manet also experimented with *plein air* painting. This was becoming much more practicable with the advent of manufactured paints in tin tubes and portable boxes such as this English example of the late 19th century.

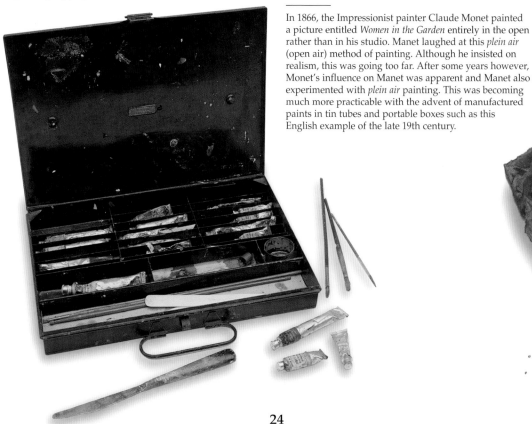

FRUITS ON A TABLE, 1864

This record of Manet's lesson in still life painting for Eva Gonzales gives a good idea of how Manet went about making a painting. *"Get it down quickly. Don't worry about the background. Just go for the tonal values. You see? When you look at it, and above all when you think how to render it as you see it, that is, in such a way that it makes the same impression on the viewer as it does on you, you don't look for, you don't see the lines on the paper over there do you? And the grapes, now do you count each grape? Of course not. What strikes you is their clear amber color, and the bloom which models the form by softening it. What you have to decide with the cloth is where the highlights come and then the planes which are not in direct light. Halftones are for the Magasin Pittoresque engravers. The folds will come by themselves if you put them in their proper place."*

POPPY SEEDS

During the 19th century, experiments with different types of oil media led to the use of oil extracted from poppy seeds. Poppy oil did not yellow as much as other types of oils, but was more difficult to extract and therefore more expensive than linseed or walnut oil, which was also available. Investigations show that Manet used both poppy and linseed oil.

25

FAMOUS IMAGES

In March 1863, Manet held an exhibition of his paintings in the gallery of art dealer Louis Martinet on the Boulevard des Italiens, which was an important venue for artists whose work failed to be accepted by the official *Salon*. Among the works to be exhibited was *Music in the Tuileries Gardens*. This was a group portrait of Manet's family and friends and effectively a snapshot of Parisian life. Theodore Duret tells us that: *"At that time the Château of the Tuileries, where the Emperor held court, was a center of opulent life which extended to the gardens. The band concerts held there twice a week attracted a sophisticated and elegant crowd."* In 1862, Manet went to the gardens almost every day, from two to four, making sketches under the trees, then returned to his studio where he planned and executed the painting. The picture is a snapshot in the photographic sense as well. The framing of the scene with figures cut in half by the edge of the canvas is reminiscent of the way in which the new medium of photography was making "instant pictures"; the flattened perspective with some areas in focus, some just a blur, also recalls the artlessness of photography.

Charles Baudelaire, poet. One of the most famous of all Manet's friends, and possibly the most influential. A strong advocate of modernity, whose poems shocked as much as Manet's paintings.

Théophile Gautier, art critic.

Henri Fantin-Latour, painter. One of Manet's earliest friends and devoted supporters.

Baron Taylor, Inspector of Museums.

Édouard Manet.

Eugene Manet, the artist's brother.

Albert de Balleroy, with whom Manet shared a studio. He specialized in painting hunting scenes.

Zacharie Astruc, artist, writer, and composer. He wrote a poem about Manet's painting *Olympia*, as well as collaborating on an illustrated song sheet with Manet.

Madame Loubens.

MUSIC IN THE TUILERIES GARDENS, 1862

Manet would lunch at the Café Tortini before making his way to the Tuileries Gardens to sketch. When he had finished, around five or six in the evening, he would return to the Café where his artist friends would be waiting to see the results of his work. This admiration was not however shared by the critics and the public. When the painting was exhibited it caused an outrage. One artist, known only as an *amateur* in this account by Émile Zola, was almost moved to violence: *"an exasperated amateur was threatening to take violent action if* Music in the Tuileries [Gardens] *was allowed to remain in the gallery. I understand the anger of the amateur: imagine under the trees of the Tuileries a whole crowd, a hundred people perhaps, who are simply bustling around in the sun; each person is simply a tache [mark], scarcely fixed, on which the details become lines or black dots. If I had been there I would have asked the amateur to stand at a respectful distance: then he would have seen that these taches were alive, that the crowd was talking..."* The painting includes portraits of many of Manet's family and friends.

Jacques Offenbach, composer. Internationally renowned for his light operettas such as *The Tales of Hoffmann.*

A LITTLE JOKE

Manet played a visual trick on his audience by painting the child's hoop after he had signed the painting. The hoop, which casually leans against a chair, also rests over the top of the artist's name.

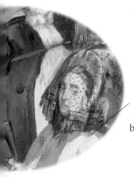

Madame Lejosne, wife of Commandant Hippolyte Lejosne in whose home Manet had been introduced to Baudelaire. He had strong Republican sympathies as well as being a supporter of the arts.

THE TRAPEZE ARTIST

In the very top left hand corner of the painting Manet has painted in a pair of legs with two tiny green shoes which belong to a trapeze artist who is cut off by the picture frame.

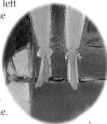

MYSTERY MAN

What many critics and art historians have tried to come to terms with is the strange perspective. The man reflected in the mirror should be standing in front of Suzon if the picture is to make sense. The bar is facing the spectator but the angle of the reflection is all wrong. The man is clearly "missing" from the viewer's side of the bar unless Manet has made a fundamental mistake and he was too experienced an artist to have done so. The conclusion is that Manet has made a deliberate error—but why?

A BAR AT THE FOLIES-BERGÈRE, 1881/82

Many different interpretations of this world famous painting exist. It is a quite straightforward picture in some senses; Suzon, the barmaid, posed for Manet in the "uniform" that she normally wore at work behind the bar. Behind her, reflected in the mirror, is depicted the balcony and audience of the Folies-Bergère along with chandeliers, Suzon's back and a male customer with top hat and cane in his left hand. She leans on the marble counter top, which is ranged with bottles, a vase with roses, and a crystal bowl holding tangerines.

A MODERN VENUS

One view is that the barmaid is a modern day Venus, the goddess of love from classical antiquity. The writer Beth Archer Brombert points to the clues; in Suzon's dress and on the bar in front of Suzon is a white rose (symbol of purity), and a pink rose (symbol of divine love). The rose was commonly associated with Venus in Renaissance art, from which Manet often drew references, because the pricking of its thorns was compared to the wounds of love.

A TRULY MODERN WOMAN

When the painting was exhibited at the *Salon*, the portrait of the barmaid received a mixed reaction. To one critic she had a *"cardboard head,"* but another described her as: *"a beautiful girl, truly alive, truly modern."* What is indisputable, however, is Suzon's complete detachment. She looks slightly down and to the left of the viewer, avoiding eye contact, trapped between the spectator and the bar on one side, and the crowd and the male customer on the other. The painting seems to be about looking, but also about the process of painting itself: what is real and what is an illusion? Is this the reason for the "missing" man? Has Manet cast us in his role?

FAMOUS IMAGES

One of the best known of Manet's paintings is *A Bar at the Folies-Bergère*. When he started the painting in 1881, his health was already failing and it was the last major work to be submitted to the Salon. In 1881, the Folies-Bergère was a center of entertainment which attracted a wide audience (it still offers nightly entertainment at 32 rue Richer).The venue was divided into a large hall with balconies and another large open area with bars. Its clientele was made up by people of all social classes. Manet visited the bars and made sketches, which were to be the basis of a studio painting. The barmaid, a model named Suzon, actually worked in the Folies-Bergère and was persuaded to pose for Manet behind a table in his studio.

NIGHTLY ENTERTAINMENT

Every evening a range of activities could be found, including circus, cabaret, acrobats, and dancers together with the offerings of a normal Parisian café.

APPLE SUBSTITUTE?

Our attention is drawn to the tangerines on the counter in front of Suzon. Is Manet playing again with his art historical "in jokes"? The orange (or tangerine) was sometimes used as a substitute for the apple from the Tree of Knowledge that Eve handed to Adam and so caused the fall from grace.

MERY LAURENT, 1881/82

This detail from the reflection of the crowd on the balcony has been identified as a mini-portrait of Manet's friend, Mery Laurent. Mery Laurent started her career in Paris as a teenager working in café cabaret. She quickly attracted a following including many artists who were mesmerized by her beauty. She was supposed to have been the model for the central character in Émile Zola's novel, *Nana*, as well as having countless poems dedicated to her and portraits painted of her. It is likely that Manet was one of a string of lovers Mery Laurent is reported to have had among the literary and artistic set in Paris.

THE AUDIENCE FOR THE PICTURES

Who was Manet painting for? He was a man of independent financial means and therefore did not rely upon patrons or depend upon income from the sale of his paintings. What motivated Manet was the desire to be recognized as an artist. In Paris at the time, that meant having work accepted by the Salon because there were only a few private galleries, and these did not carry the same stamp of approval as the *Salon*. The problem was that Manet was so convinced that his way of painting was right that his pictures were continually refused by the *Salon*. In 1863, thousands of paintings were turned down by the Salon and a compromise was reached: a separate exhibition of refused paintings would be held at the same time. This separate exhibition, known as the *Salon des Refusés*, included Manet's *Le Déjeuner sur l'Herbe*.

THE BATTLE OF THE KEARSAGE AND ALABAMA, 1864

When the American civil war reached as far as the French coast, all of France took notice. The sea battle off Cherbourg between the Unionist corvette *Kearsage* and the Confederate *Alabama* was a newsworthy event, which Manet is reported to have witnessed at close hand. The painting was displayed in the window of a Paris art dealer where it attracted a great deal of attention, not all favorable. This was, however, an opportunity for the public to view the event in an age before the widespread coverage of photography and film.

THE ESCAPE OF ROCHEFORT, 1880/81

When Manet decided to paint a history painting (from the French, *histoire*, meaning story) about the escape of Henri Rochefort, he was effectively demonstrating to his audience his support for the Republic and his distaste for the Emperor. Rochefort had been a leading figure in the Communards and had been sentenced to life imprisonment in New Caledonia (an island in the Pacific). In 1874, he had made a dramatic escape and lived in Geneva until the French government amnesty of 1880. Rochefort himself supplied details of the escape for Manet to base the painting on. Rochefort and his supporters were enthusiastic about the picture but not surprisingly Manet decided against submitting it to the Salon.

A MEETING OF THE JUDGES OF THE SALON DES ARTISTES FRANÇAIS, 1885 *Henri Gervex*

The procedure that decided which paintings were accepted was a long-standing one. A jury of 24 established academic painters, all men of course, stood in a group and voted paintings in (by raising a hand) or out. In 1867, Manet decided he could no longer bear the rejection of these conservative judges and planned his own exhibition. He borrowed 18,000 francs from his mother and built an exhibition space on the corner of Avenue Montaigne, which housed 53 paintings. Manet's catalog for the exhibition was prefaced with "Reasons for a Private Exhibition." It went on to say: "... *people have protested, because there is a traditional system of teaching... in painting, and because those who have been brought up according to such principles do not acknowledge any other... it is now only a question for the painter of gaining the goodwill of the public which has been turned into a would-be enemy."*

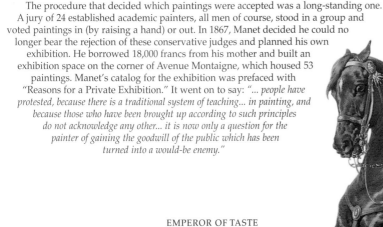

EMPEROR OF TASTE

It is said that when the Salon rejected so many paintings in 1863, the thousands of unhappy artists complained bitterly to the government. In desperation Emperor Napoleon was asked to intervene and he visited the Salon in person. Being unable to distinguish between those paintings that the jury had accepted and those they had refused, he ordered a separate exhibition to run alongside the official exhibition. This may not have pleased everyone, because many artists took offence and withdrew their paintings completely.

WHAT THE CRITICS SAY

Manet wrote a letter to Baudelaire shortly after the opening of the 1865 Salon, which exhibited his paintings of *Olympia* and *Jesus Mocked by Soldiers*. The letter began: *"I wish I had you here, my dear Baudelaire, insults are beating down on me like hail, I've never been through anything like it... I wish I could have your sound judgement on my pictures because all this uproar is upsetting, and obviously something must be wrong."*

Manet was truly hurt by the torrent of abuse that followed the display of his work in the 1865 Salon and at other exhibitions. He wanted to be popular but his style of painting was always going to attract criticism. Baudelaire's reply was swift and harsh. Any true artist must not be concerned with the opinions of the critics and must have self belief.

"So I must speak to you of yourself," wrote Baudelaire: *"I must try to show you what you are worth. What you demand is really stupid."*

SIR FREDERICK LEIGHTON

Leighton was an English artist and president of the Royal Academy of Art in London. His academy style was completely at odds with Manet's own. In 1878, Leighton visited Manet in his studio and commented on Manet's picture *The Skating Rink* saying: *"It's very good but... don't you think the outlines are not well enough defined?"* Manet records, that: *"he realized he was annoying me and went away."*

Nausicaa (detail).

THE ARTIST'S CHAMPION

Charles Baudelaire was probably the most important figure in the development of Manet's art, and Manet looked continually to him for support. They had been friends since the 1850s, and continued to be close until Baudelaire's death in 1867. Baudelaire was a "modern" poet who sought "modern beauty" in his poetry.

PORTRAIT OF ÉMILE ZOLA, 1868

Zola was a great supporter of Manet and critic of the Salon system. He wrote for a weekly publication called *L'Evenement* which on May 7, 1866, included an article by Zola on Manet. He wrote *"It appears that I am the first to praise Manet without reservation. This is because I care little for all those boudoir paintings... those miserable canvases wherein I find nothing alive... I am so sure that Manet will be one of the masters of tomorrow that I should believe I had made a good bargain, had I the money, in buying all his canvases today."* Zola's view of the Salon jury was forthright: *"it hacks at art and offers the crowd only the mutilated corpse."* It was with Zola's encouragement that Manet took the brave step of paying for a private exhibition of his work in 1867.

THE ABUSED CRITIC

Jules Champfleury was a writer and critic and a good friend of Manet. Champfleury championed the Realist movement and was portrayed with Manet and other friends such as Baudelaire in Fantin-Latour's group portrait *Homage to Delacroix*. Champfleury was himself criticized for his association with the Realist artists and found himself caricatured in the popular press.

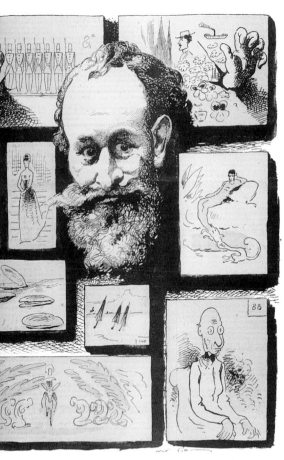

MANET RIDICULED

The cover of this satirical paper dated May 11, 1876, shows a caricature of Édouard Manet, his head and hands poking through a hanging of paintings, presumably referring to the exhibition at the annual Salon. *L'Éclipse* ridiculed Manet in the 1860s when he submitted his paintings to the Salon, and a decade later it was still ridiculing him. An article of the time is to the point. *"It is true, entirely true, that Manet has almost unanimously been rejected..."* When the jury came to examine his paintings, one of the members exclaimed, *"Enough of this. We have allowed Manet ten years to turn over a new leaf. He hasn't done so... reject him!"*

THE DUEL

Manet was in a furious mood after the critic Duranty had written a slightly critical appraisal of two of his paintings. He slapped Duranty on the face, which was, as every gentleman knows, a challenge to a duel. The two men met in the forest of Saint Germain at 11am and fought with swords until Duranty was wounded. Fortunately the seconds declared honor was satisfied and the two men, rather relieved, made up.

A LASTING IMPRESSION

Manet died on April 30, 1883, aged 51. He had been suffering for some time from the final stages of syphilis causing him constant pain and gangrene in his left foot, which was amputated 11 days before his death. Claude Monet, Antonin Proust, Émile Zola, Edgar Degas, and Jacques-Émile Blanche all attended the funeral. Blanche is reported to have heard Degas say *"he was greater than we thought."* This is a fitting epitaph for an artist whose influence on the course of 19th-century art was profound. Today we first think of the Impressionists as the group who made the break from the traditional studio bound art of the time, but it was Manet who made it possible. He was the bridge between the old schools and the new. Manet's obsession with painting what he saw, the truth of the modern world, broke new ground for those who followed.

THE FIGURE IN FOCUS

Manet made many full length studies of figures such as *The Tragic Actor, The Beggar, The Rag Picker,* and *The Fifer.* His style, which was heavily criticized in his lifetime, was to portray the figure against a flat, neutral background. The figure appeared to be carefully, almost artificially, lit which had the effect of pushing it forward out of the background. His advice was *"In a figure, look for the full light and the full shadow, the rest will follow."* In this detail from The Fifer, 1886 (shown here) Manet paints the boy in exactly this way with only a hint of shadow behind his feet to anchor him into the neutral background, which also serves to sharpen or "focus" attention onto the figure.

FASHION PHOTOGRAPHY

Manet's eye was very like the modern studio photographer's eye which also carefully arranges the lighting on the figure emphasizing contrast and losing half tones. Today photographers make use of artificial backgrounds in exactly the way Manet did. The neutral flat backdrop serves to focus the viewer onto the subject and make the figure stand out.

LE DÉJEUNER SUR L'HERBE

Pablo Picasso

Manet's painting of the luncheon on the grass was like an earthquake in the art world; the aftershocks continued for many years. Picasso made this painting on the subject in 1960, nearly 100 years after Manet's version.

BOW WOW WOW

The power of Manet's *Le Déjeuner sur l'Herbe* (left and on pages 18 & 19) has not been lost on those who followed. The allusions which were so full of scandalous meaning in Manet's time might not stir such emotions today but nevertheless the composition has been carefully copied for many different purposes. Even the more recent versions present an image which seems to carry some promise of disrepute; for example, it was used on the cover of pop group Bow Wow Wow's 1981 album *Go Wild in the Country*.

DID YOU KNOW?
FASCINATING FACTS ABOUT THE ARTIST
AND THE TIMES IN WHICH HE WORKED

• Although he never exhibited with the Impressionists, all of them recognized Manet as their leader although he never felt he should be. In cafés and at their homes, he regularly led discussions about new ideas of art, which inspired them all.

• Manet was very popular. He spoke softly and apart from the duel with Duranty, rarely argued with others. He enjoyed the fashionable life of Paris, dressing elegantly and spending time in the smartest cafés and mixing with high society.

• Manet's parents were well-respected members of the bourgeoisie and they hoped that their eldest son would become a lawyer. They were disappointed when he insisted he wanted to be an artist.

• Initially, to please his parents, in 1848 Manet agreed to join the French Navy as a sea cadet. He sailed to South America when he was sixteen, but he later failed his naval examinations and so returned home to become an artist.

• Although attacked by critics throughout his life, Manet was hurt and confused—he thought he was following in the footsteps of a long line of great artists and he continued to hope for recognition and acceptance throughout his life.

• The Salon des Refusés was held in the spring of 1863 and never again. It took place because that year over half of the 5000 paintings submitted to the official Salon jury were refused. The rejected artists complained so angrily that the Emperor Napoleon III ordered a special exhibition where they could display their works and

give people a chance to make up their own mind about whether the jury was correct or not. Napoleon thought that the public would agree with the Salon jury, but instead, it showed how narrow-minded they were and how many artists had new, interesting ideas that were being overlooked.

- Conventional painters created fine gradations of tone, from dark to light, but Manet painted dramatic contrasts, so his images look sharp and flat. This angered contemporary critics as artists were expected to spend years perfecting the technique of blending light and shadows.

- *Olympia* was considered far more shocking than a traditional nude in a painting, partly because she had some clothes on! The slippers, choker, bangle, orchid in her hair, and the shawl shrugged off beneath her, were symbols of adornment that showed she was trying to look attractive rather than be demure as people believed women should be.

- From about 1876, a table was kept reserved for Manet at the Café de la Nouvelle Athènes in Paris where he spent many hours each week, discussing new ideas about art with other artists.

- Despite many of his paintings being quite shocking, Manet's fear of offending the art authorities remained with him throughout his life. In 1876, when he was asked by some students from the official Parisian art academy, the École des Beaux-Arts, to teach them he refused, fearing that the Academy would not approve.

- Largely through his friendship with Berthe Morisot, Manet's work became freer and more fluid after the 1870s, but although they remained good friends throughout their lives, Manet never painted Morisot again after her marriage to his brother in 1874.

- Like many of the other young, avant-garde artists, Manet became inspired by Japanese prints and many of his compositions reflect this.

- From about 1873, Manet's palette brightened progressively, but he never lost his love of black that he had learned to use from the Spanish artists.

- Monet encouraged Manet to paint in the open air rather than always in a studio and from 1874, they painted together in Argenteuil just outside Paris. In 1878, before Monet became rich and successful, Manet lent him 1000 francs.

- In 1881, just two years before he died, Manet was awarded the Légion d'Honneur, a medal in official recognition of his work. Although he was honored, he said it "had come too late to repair twenty years' lack of success."

- When Manet died, Monet started a fund to raise money so that poor Madame Manet did not have to sell *Olympia* to make ends meet.

SUMMARY TIMELINE OF
THE ARTIST & HIS CONTEMPORARIES

THE LIFE OF MANET

~1832~

In the year that Manet is born, Gustave Doré, the engraver, illustrator, and sculptor is born in Strasbourg—both men also die in the same year

~1833~

The artist Paul Delaroche paints *The Execution of Lady Jane Grey*

~1834~

The artists Edgar Degas, J.A.M. Whistler and the poet, artist, and designer William Morris are born; in London, the Palace of Westminster is destroyed by fire and J.M.W. Turner leaves his dinner to sketch it

~1835~

The Japanese Ukiyo-e artist Hokusai produces his *Hundred Views of Mount Fuji*

~1837~

Queen Victoria ascends the British throne; the English painter John Constable dies

~1839~

Photography is invented; Cézanne is born; John Martin paints *The Coronation of Queen Victoria* and Théodore Chassériau paints *Vénus Anadymone*

~1840~

The Romantic painter Caspar David Friedrich dies; Queen Victoria marries Prince Albert and artists Claude Monet, Odilon Redon, and Auguste Rodin are born

~1841~

Auguste Renoir, Berthe Morisot, and Frédéric Bazille are born; the Scottish artist David Wilkie dies; a huge marble statue of George Washington by American sculptor Horatio Greenough, based on the Greek god Zeus is unveiled in Washington, D.C.

~1844~

The naïve artist Henri Rousseau and the painter, sculptor, and photographer Thomas Eakins are born; Turner paints *Rain, Steam, and Speed*

~1845~

The Irish Famine begins, lasting until 1852

~1847~

Thomas Couture paints *The Romans of the Decadence*

~1848~

In "The Year of Revolutions," political revolutions take place across Europe; the French artist Paul Gauguin and American glass designer Louis Comfort Tiffany are born; Manet sails to Rio de Janeiro with the navy

~1849~

The artist John William Waterhouse is born; Dante Gabriel Rossetti paints *The Girlhood of Mary Virgin*; the California Gold Rush begins

~1850~

Manet enters the studio of Thomas Couture and also studies at the Academie Suisse in the evenings

~1851~

The Great Exhibition is opened by Queen Victoria in London, in a massive glass building known as the Crystal Palace— six million people visit between May and September

~1853~
Vincent van Gogh is born;
William Holman Hunt paints
The Awakening Conscience

~1855~
Manet visits Italy and makes
copies of the Old Masters; Courbet
paints *The Painter's Studio*

~1856~
Manet leaves Couture's studio
and travels extensively; Ingres
paints *Madame Moitessier*; the
artist John Singer Sargent is born

~1857~
An earthquake in Tokyo, Japan
kills over 100,000; another in
Naples, Italy kills 11000;
Hollywood is founded; Jean-
François Millet paints
The Gleaners

~1859~
The Pointillist artist Georges
Seurat is born; *The Origin of Species*
by Charles Darwin is published;
Manet submits *The Absinthe
Drinker to the Salon*, but is
rejected and he becomes friends
with the poet Charles Baudelaire

~1861~
Manet's painting *The Guitar
Player* is accepted by the Salon
and he becomes friends with
Edgar Degas; the American
Civil War begins

~1863~
The year of the Salon des
Refusés; Alexandre Cabanel
paints *The Birth of Venus*

~1864~
Henri Fantin-Latour paints
Homage to Delacroix

~1865~
In the year that *Olympia*
provokes outrage at the Salon,
Manet meets Cézanne and
Monet; the American Civil
War ends

~1866~
Zola publishes an article on
Manet, describing him as the
greatest modern master;
Russian artist Wassily
Kandinsky is born; Monet
paints *Women in the Garden*

~1867~
Das Kapital the Communist
"bible" written by Karl
Marx is published

~1868~
Manet visits England briefly
and meets Berthe Morisot

~1870~
The Franco-Prussian War
begins, lasting until 1871,
Manet serves with Degas in the
artillery of the National Guard

~1874~
The first Impressionist
exhibition is held; Manet paints
with Monet at Argenteuil;
Degas paints *The Dance Class*;

Whistler begins *Nocturne in
Black and Gold: the Falling
Rocket*; Renoir paints *La Loge*
and Gustave Moreau begins
The Apparition

~1875~
Manet visits Venice

~1876~
Alexander Graham
Bell invents the telephone;
the second Impressionist
exhibition is held; Courbet
dies and the sculptor
Constantin Brancusi
and painter Maurice de
Vlaminck are born

~1878~
Frederick Leighton visits
Manet and comments on
his work, that year he also
paints *Nausicaa*

~1879~
The artists Paul Klee and
Francis Picabia are born;
Manet's former teacher
Couture dies; Manet's
fatal illness begins

~1881~
Pablo Picasso is born;
Manet is awarded the Légion
d'Honneur

~1883~
In the year that Manet dies,
Antoni Gaudí begins building
the Sagrada Família Cathedral
in Barcelona, Spain and Coco
Chanel is born

WHAT DID HE SAY?

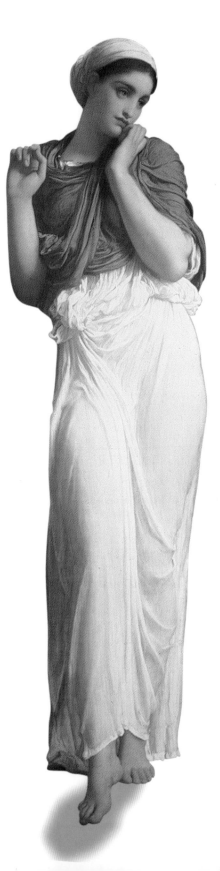

Here are some things that Manet said or wrote:

• "Black is not a color"

• "Color is a matter of taste and of sensitivity"

• "I need to work to feel well"

• "I paint what I see and not what others like to see"

• "No one can be a painter unless he cares for painting above all else"

• "The attacks of which I have been the object have broken the spring of life in me... People don't realize what it feels like to be constantly insulted"

• "It is not enough to know your craft—you have to have feeling. Science is all very well, but for us imagination is worth far more"

• "There are no lines in nature, only areas of color, one against another"

• "There is only one true thing: instantly paint what you see. When you've got it, you've got it. When you haven't, you begin again. All the rest is humbug"

• (About Berthe Morisot) "This woman's work is exceptional. Too bad she's not a man"

• (About Velazquez) "He is the painter of painters"

• "You would hardly believe how difficult it is to place a figure alone on a canvas and to concentrate all the interest on this single and universal figure and still keep it living and real"

• "There's no symmetry in nature. One eye is never exactly the same as the other. There's always a difference. We all have a more or less crooked nose and an irregular mouth"

A WORK IN CLOSE-UP

This painting has been the subject of a great deal of discussion and historians still question its meaning. It is a scene of everyday life, featuring food and drink— a theme that Manet returned to throughout his career, but it goes against conventional rules and expectations of paintings. The main characters seem to ignore each other and their faces are inexpressive.

The central three-quarter length, smart young man is sixteen-year-old Léon Leenhoff, the illegitimate son of Manet's wife and probably Manet's son as well.

The work could be a tribute to Dutch art—both Léon and Suzanne were Dutch-born. The dark interior and the detailed still life of open oysters, peeled lemon, and a knife on the table are similar to 17th century Dutch painting.

X-rays show that large studio windows with metal framing bars once ran across the background, but Manet has adjusted the scene to create a bourgeois dining room.

Another still life of antique swords and a helmet on a chair is livened up with a cat casually grooming itself.

The man smoking is the painter Auguste Rousselin, an old friend of Manet's. He gazes across the room—viewers are not shown what he is looking at.

The maid stands frozen, a coffee pot in her hand next to a large potted plant as Léon strides away.

Breakfast in the Studio or The Luncheon, 1868, oil on canvas, 46 x 60 in/118.3 x 154 cm, *New Pinakothek, Munich, Germany*

WHERE TO SEE THIS ARTIST'S WORKS IN THE USA

There are plenty of places across the USA where you can enjoy Manet's work. Below are some of them. Always check with the gallery or museum that the work is on display before visiting.

The Art Institute of Chicago
(www.artic.edu)

Detroit Institute of Arts, Michigan
(www.dia.org)

Fine Arts Museums of San Francisco, California
(search.famsf.org)

J. Paul Getty Museum, Los Angeles, California
(www.getty.edu)

The Metropolitan Museum, New York, New York
(www.metmuseum.org)

Museum of Fine Arts Houston, Texas
(www.mfah.org)

Museum of Fine Arts Boston, Massachusetts
(www.mfa.org)

National Gallery of Art, Washington D.C.
(www.nga.gov)

Norton Simon Museum, California
(www.nortonsimon.org)

Yale University Art Gallery, Connecticut
(artgallery.yale.edu)

Cleveland Museum of Art, Ohio
(www.clemusart.com)

Cincinnati Art Museum, Ohio
(cincinnatiartmuseum.org)

Frick Collection, New York
(www.frick.org)

Harvard University Art Museums, Massachusetts
(www.artmuseums. harvard.edu)

Hill-Stead Museum, Connecticut
(www.hillstead.org)

Kimbell Art Museum, Texas
(www.kimbellart.org)

Minneapolis Institute of Art, Minnesota, Minneapolis
(www.artsmia.org)

Philadelphia Museum of Art, Pennsylvania
(www.philamuseum.org)

Pomona College Museum of Art, California
(web4.campus.pomona.edu)

Princeton University Art Museum, New Jersey
(mcis2.princeton.edu)

Rhode Island School of Design Museum of Art, Rhode Island
(www.risdmuseum.org)

Saint Louis Art Museum, Missouri
(stlouis.art.museum)

San Diego Museum of Art, California
(www.sdmart.org)

The Barnes Foundation, Pennsylvania
(www.barnesfoundation.org)

Virginia Museum of Fine Arts, Richmond, Virginia
(www.vmfa.state.va.us)

WHERE TO SEE THIS ARTIST'S WORKS IN THE REST OF THE WORLD

Many works by Manet are in the collections of museums and galleries around the world, particularly in Europe, but check before you visit to make sure that the work you are hoping to see is on display.

The State
Hermitage Museum,
St. Petersburg, Russia
(www.hermitagemuseum.org)

Musée d'Orsay,
Paris, France
(www.musee-orsay.fr)

The National Gallery,
London, UK
(www.nationalgallery.org.uk)

Neue Pinakothek,
Munich, Germany
(www.pinakothek.de)

Rijksmuseum,
Amsterdam,
The Netherlands
(www.rijksmuseum.nl)

Städel Museum,
Frankfurt, Germany
(www.staedelmuseum.de)

Ashmolean Museum at the
University of Oxford,
Oxford, UK
(www.ashmolean.org)

Courtauld Institute of Art,
London, UK
(www.courtauld.ac.uk)

E.G. Bührle Collection,
Zurich, Switzerland
(www.buehrle.ch)

Kunsthalle Mannheim,
Mannheim, Germany
(www.kunsthalle-mannheim.eu)

Musée des Beaux-
Arts de Lyon,
France
(www.mba-lyon.fr)

Museo Nacional
de Bellas Artes,
Buenos Aires, Argentina
(www.mnba.org.ar)

Museu Calouste
Gulbenkian,
Lisbon, Portugal
(museu.gulbenkian.pt)

Museu de Arte
de São Paulo,
Brazil
(www.uol.com.br)

National Gallery
of Victoria,
Australia
(www.ngv.vic.gov.au)

National Museum
of Western Art,
Tokyo, Japan
(www.nmwa.go.jp)

National Museum
and Galleries of Wales,
Cardiff, UK
(www.museumwales.ac.uk)

New Carlsberg Glyptotek,
Copenhagen, Denmark
(www.glyptoteket.dk)

Oskar Reinhart Collection,
Switzerland
(www.roemerholz.ch)

Österreichische
Galerie Belvedere,
Vienna, Austria
(www.belvedere.at)

The Ordrupgaard
Collection,
Charlottenlund, Denmark
(www.ordrupgaard.dk)

Van Gogh Museum,
Amsterdam, The
Netherlands
(www.vangoghmuseum.nl)

Thyssen-Bornemisza
Museum,
Madrid, Spain
(www.museothyssen.org)

Von der Heydt-Museum,
Wuppertal, Germany
(www.von-der-heydt-museum.de)

Wallraf-Richartz-Museum,
Cologne, Germany
(www.museenkoeln.de)

FURTHER READING & WEBSITES

BOOKS

Edouard Manet
(Meet the Artist),
Melody S. Mis,
Powerkids·Press, 2007

Manet (Eyewitness
Guides),
Patricia Wright,
Dorling Kindersley, 2000

Favourite Classic Artists,
Liz Gogerly,
Wayland, 2007

Manet
(Art Profiles for Kids),
Kathleen Tracy,
Mitchell Lane Publishing,
2009

Start Exploring
Masterpieces: A Fact Filled
Colouring Book,
Steven Zorn,
Running Press, US, 2000

Color your own
Manet Paintings,
Marty Noble,
Dover Publications Inc,
2008

Manet to Picasso
(National Gallery
Company),
C. Riopelle,
Yale University Press, 2006

Discovering Great Artists,
MaryAnn F. Kohl,
Kim Solga,
Brilliant Publications, 2003

Manet (World's
Great Artists Series),
Sandra Stotksy,
Nathaniel Harris,
Parragon Plus, 1994

Impressionism
(Eyewitness Guides),
Jude Welton,
Dorling Kindersley, 2000

Impressionism
(The World's Greatest Art),
Tamsin Pickeral,
Flame Tree, 2007

Impressionism
(Art Revolutions),
Linda Bolton,
Belitha Press Ltd, 2003

WEBSITES

www.ibiblio.org/wm/paint/
auth/manet/

www.abcgallery.com/M/
manet/manet.html

www.nga.gov/collection/
gallery/gg90/gg90-
main1.html

www.nationalgallery.org.uk
/artists/edouard-manet

www.edouardmanet.com/t
heframe.html
www.musee-
orsay.fr/index.php?id=851&
L=1&tx_commentaire_pi1[s
howUid]=7087&no_cache=1

www.musee-orsay.fr/
en/collections/works-in-
focus/search/commentaire/
commentaire_id/emile-
zola-313.html?no_cache=1

www.manetedouard.org/

www.renoirinc.com/biogra
phy/artists/manet.htm

www.nga.gov/collection/
railwel.shtm

www.guggenheim
collection.org/site/artist_
bio_96.html

www.philamuseum.org/
micro_sites/exhibitions/
manet/kids/home.html

www.philamuseum.org/
micro_sites/exhibitions/
manet/gallery/manet/
manet.htm

www.impressionniste.net/
manet_edouard.htm

www.artlex.com/ArtLex/
ij/impressionism.
Pissarro.html

GLOSSARY

Avant-garde—a person or group who is at the forefront of new ideas and techniques, especially in the arts

Bourgeois/Bourgeoisie—the middle class

Draughtsman—a person skilled at drawing

Gradations—gradual changes usually in tones

Engraving—mainly describes a method of printing where lines are cut or etched on to a metal plate and ink transferred from the grooves on to paper

Légion d' Honneur—an award of high distinction given by the French Republic to a French person who has made outstanding achievements in military or civil life

Naïve—simple, childlike style

Romanticism—Romantic art was concerned with the expression of feelings and was at its height at the beginning of the 19th century, particularly with artists such as Delacroix

Tache—a brushstroke which leaves a broad square or oblong stroke of paint and is not smoothed into

the surface. Impressionists often painted quickly to create an "impression" of a scene and painted in large taches

Titian—a 16th century artist who is sometimes called the founder of modern painting. He painted in a free style, using patches of color and sometimes put the paint on with his fingers rather than a brush. The Impressionist style is often compared to his work

Ukiyo-e—means "pictures of the floating world" in Japanese and describes a style of Japanese woodblock prints and paintings produced

between the 17th and 20th centuries

Values—in painting, "values" refer to the tonal gradations from light to dark. A "tonal value" is the comparative darkness or lightness of a color

Venus—the Roman goddess of love who evolved from the Greek goddess Aphrodite, the mother of Cupid. The portrayal of the female nude in art is often referred to as Venus, but does not always have a particular link to the Roman myth

INDEX

ACKNOWLEDGMENTS

Picture Credits t=top, b=bottom, c=center, l=left, r=right, OFC=outside front cover.

Photo © AKG London; 6/7cb, 8tl, 29tr. © BMG Entertainment International UK & Ireland; 35b. Copyright © British Museum; 19br. © Bibliothèque Nationale of France, Paris; 13t. Outfit by Caroline Charles, London; 34bl. Chateau de Compiegne, Oise/Lauros-Giraudon/Bridgeman Art Library, London; 21bl. Collections Royal Army Museum, Brussels; 20tl, 20cl. Courtauld Gallery, London/Bridgeman Art Library, London; 28. Mary Evans Picture Library; 7tl, 7tr, 8b, 33cl. Galleria degli Uffizi, Florence. Photo © AKG London; 22bl. Highgate Cemetery, London/Bridgeman Art Library, London; 6/7c. Kunsthalle, Hamburg. Photo © AKG London; 23tr. Le Déjeuner sur L'Herbe, 1960, Pablo Picasso © Succession Picasso/DACS 1997 (Private Collection. Photo © AKG London); 35t. A Meeting of the Judges of the Salon des Artistes Francais, 1885, Henri Gervex © ADAGP, Paris and DACS, London 1997 (Musee d'Orsay, Paris, France/Peter Willi/Bridgeman Art Library, London); 31t. Musee d'Orsay, Paris. Photo © AKG London; 9br, 30br. Musee d'Orsay, Paris. Photo © AKG London/Erich Lessing; 10cl & 32br & 33tr, 10bl, 12tl, 12/13c, 14tr, 15cr, 15br, 17bl & 22cr, 25t, 33tl, 34cl. Musee d'Orsay, Paris, France/Giraudon/Bridgeman Art Library, London; OFC (main image), OFCt, OFCc, 10tr. Musee des Beaux-Arts, Nancy. Photo © AKG London; 29br. Musee du Louvre, Paris. Photo © AKG London; 11bl. Musee du Louvre, Paris. Photo © AKG London/Erich Lessing; 17tl & 18/19c & 35cl. Museo del Prado, Madrid. Photo © AKG London/Erich Lessing; 20bl. Museum of Art, Philadelphia. Photo © AKG London; 30cl. Museum of Fine Arts, Boston, Massachusetts/Bridgeman Art Library, London; 16bl. Gare Saint-Lazare, Gift of Horace Havemeyer in memory of his mother, Louisine W. Havemeyer, © 1997 Board of Trustees, National Gallery of Art, Washington, 1873, oil on canvas, .933 x 1.115 (36¼ x 43⅞); framed: 1.130 x 1.327 x .053 (44½ x 52¼ x 2⅛); 17cr and detail 17cl. National Gallery, London/Bridgeman Art Library, London; 26/27. National Maritime Museum, London; 7c. National Portrait Gallery, London. Photo © AKG London; 6bl. Neue Pinakothek, Munich. Photo © AKG London; 11tr. Städtische Kunsthalle, Mannheine, photo © AKG London/Erich Lessing; 20/21ct. Private Collection. Photo © AKG London; 32l. Private Collection/Giraudon/Bridgeman Art Library, London; 15cl. Private Collection/Photo © Christie's Images/The Bridgeman Art Library; OFCb. Pushkin Museum, Moscow. Photo © AKG London; 12bl. The Royal Collection, London. Photo © AKG London; 31br. Szepmuveszeti Muzeum, Budapest. Photo © AKG London; 9tl.

NOTE TO READERS
The website addresses are correct at the time of publishing. However, due to
the ever-changing nature of the Internet, websites and content may change.
Some websites can contain links that are unsuitable for children. The publisher
is not responsible for changes in content or website addresses. We advise
that Internet searches should be supervised by an adult.